EXPLORING
The God Question

LEADER'S MANUAL

written by

IAIN MORRIS

for use in conjunction with
The God Question DVD series and Study Guide

Published by Search For Truth Enterprises Ltd
www.searchfortruthenterprises.com

Edition 1 – *EXPLORING The God Question – Leader's Manual*

ISBN 978-0-9576023-1-1

Author – Iain Morris
Iain Morris' professional life encompasses the worlds of education and television and film production. He produced and directed this series of films. He is also a member of the board of the Search For Truth Charitable Trust.

Typeset, Designed and Distributed by:
Sanctus Media Ltd
Bo'ness
Tel: 01506 827217
www.sanctusmedia.com

See inside back pages for image copyright credits

Search for Truth Enterprises Ltd (Company No: SC344477)
is a subsidiary of Search for Truth Charitable Trust

Search for Truth Charitable Trust (Charity No: SC039465. Company No: SC340300) is a registered charity and private limited company registered in Scotland

WELCOME TO THE GOD QUESTION SERIES!

Your role as leader will be crucial not only to the success of the discussion, but to the group's whole experience of using the series. This Leader's Manual has been produced to help you and your group members gain as much from the sessions as possible.

It provides you, the leader, with:
- additional information on the series and why it was produced
- support in introducing the topics to your group
- helpful summaries for use before and after viewing
- aims for each session
- advice on how to get maximum value from each discussion

Some of the additional information in the Leader's Manual is intended to be shared with group members; other aspects of content are specific points of advice to you as group leader. **Each group member, including the leader, should have access to a Study Guide.**

THE GOD QUESTION SERIES: BROADCAST TV AND DVD

The God Question series exists in two formats:

- Three full-length documentary TV programmes entitled "THE GOD QUESTION"

   The question of God's existence attracts almost universal interest. It is a subject of colossal importance to most. The fact that it cannot be proven either way ensures ongoing debate.

   To respond to that interest, a version of the series has been produced for broadcast television and is being promoted by an international distributor.

- Six half-hour DVD programmes entitled "EXPLORING THE GOD QUESTION" – especially designed to encourage investigation and discussion

   The DVD series "Exploring The God Question" is broadly similar to the broadcast series but has some significant variations. It has been designed to encourage and support more in-depth engagement with the content of the programmes.

THE PROGRAMMES

There are three documentary programmes with accompanying Study Guide and Leader's Manual. Each programme is divided into two parts of around thirty minutes. (Parts 1 and 2 of programme 2 are a little longer.)

1 EXPLORING THE GOD QUESTION
The Cosmos (Parts 1 and 2)

2 EXPLORING THE GOD QUESTION
Life and Evolution (Parts 1 and 2)

3 EXPLORING THE GOD QUESTION
Mind and Consciousness (Parts 1 and 2)

If feasible, leaders should preview the programmes.

THE AUDIENCE

The intended audience for the series comprises people of faith as well as people of no religious faith – indeed any who are searching. They are likely to have an interest in truth rather than choosing to maintain a position without testing its validity.

People of faith might wonder 'how does my faith stand up in the face of contemporary science?' This series offers them a journey into discovering the answers for themselves.

Some believers might also find themselves in discussion with non-believers about the existence of God, with science often being the axis on which the debate spins. Viewing this series ought to be a vital source of information and experience of the key debating points.

Often people who profess no specific faith are interested in 'the God question'. The programmes are equally relevant to them.

For everyone, the discussion group format should support exploration of the key ideas.

The ultimate aim is that conclusions would be based on accurate knowledge and clear thinking.

WHAT IS AT STAKE IN THIS SERIES

...is whether the most up to date and informed understanding of the universe and life on earth, points either to the involvement of a creator or a series of chance happenings independent of a creator.

EXPLORING THE GOD QUESTION: AN INTRODUCTION

This series encourages a thoughtful evidence-based search for truth about God particularly in the light of what modern science is revealing about:

- the origin of the universe (programme 1)
- the development of life on earth (programme 2)
- the sophistication of the human mind and brain (programme 3)

These topics provide the evidence on which Exploring The God Question is based.

A unique feature of the series is that the evidence is evaluated and interpreted by believers and non-believers. Every attempt therefore is made to be scrupulously open, honest and free of propaganda. Belief should be founded on evidence and truth, as far as it can be ascertained.

WHY THIS SERIES IS IMPORTANT

Christianity is the largest religion in the world – and growing. Yet in the Western world, it appears to be in decline – a trend fostered by secularism and frequent attacks on belief in God, often launched by the New Atheists* through various media.

Some of the criticism is aimed at the dangers and damage associated with religion but of far greater significance is the claim that belief in God has no rational foundation and that 'faith' is a way of saying "we have no evidence".

Religion has been - and, some would argue, still is - a powerful influence on society. If its structures are merely propped up on the shaky foundations of superstitions, culture and make-believe, then it is time for the 'faithful' to waken up to the greatest deception of all time. On the other hand, if there is a supernatural reality we call 'God', it is the most significant fact in the universe.

Most people have a view about God. Yet perhaps for the majority, belief or non-belief is either instinctive or the product of upbringing. Only a minority is likely to have thought through the issues carefully.

Oxford Professor, Peter Atkins, declares in this series that The God Question *".. is the biggest question of all"*. If he is right, that in itself is a sufficient reason to produce this series. But there are more...

In the last few years, the subject of God's existence has been a 'hot topic'. Sometimes fierce debate is triggered by an eminent scientist such as Stephen Hawking declaring, for example, that the existence of the laws of physics make God unnecessary. The publication of books such as the late Christopher Hitchens' "God is not Great" or Richard Dawkins' "The God Delusion" is guaranteed to raise the temperature in the debate. When concepts like 'Creationism' or 'Intelligent Design' surface, a storm of protest is unleashed by some members of the scientific establishment.

Much of the ensuing debate communicates a conflict between science and belief in God. But arguably the real battle is between atheism and theism. Science itself is neutral. **This series invites viewers to see that the crucial issue is not 'science versus religion' but how scientific evidence is interpreted.**

On 'the street', there is a stereotypical view that science and religion are irreconcilable. In the very public debate about God, science is often assumed to be a thinking person's alternative. **This series tests the thesis that belief in a creator is intellectually weak and scientifically naïve.**

For many, the God issue is an emotional one. It evokes strong feelings and arouses passion, sometimes without being based on evidence that has been well thought through. In some cases, a conclusion might be based on just one piece of evidence. **This series provides an opportunity to encounter a wide range of evidence on which the issues about God's existence can be argued.**

The programmes have been produced to examine contemporary scientific understanding about *the cosmos, the origin of life* and *mind and consciousness* in an attempt to investigate if orthodox science is more convincingly interpreted as evidence for or against the existence of a creator.

---

*New Atheists: a term which has arisen to describe a number of prominent campaigners against religion and belief in God. Notably, they include Richard Dawkins, Sam Harris, Daniel Dennett and the late Christopher Hitchens.

You should find that the programmes are:

PROVOCATIVE
Viewers of any persuasion will find plenty with which they agree and disagree. Most people enjoy the comfort of hearing their own views reinforced but, in this series, the real reward may be reserved for those who are prepared to engage with points of view that they find challenging or even disturbing.

HOLISTIC
Often, arguments about God's existence are narrowly focused on one controversial issue such as evolution. There is much more to the agenda – and that is reflected in the breadth of the series.

OPEN-ENDED AND IMPARTIAL
Viewers are encouraged to draw their own conclusions. Each programme presents evidence relevant to the theme. Theists and atheists interpret the evidence in different ways but it is ultimately for the viewer to decide where the evidence leads.

FOR EVERYONE
The God Question is not propaganda. It is a genuine search for truth which presents contrasting and varied points of view for evaluation by the viewer. Although some of the ideas and concepts might be challenging to understand, every attempt has been made to make them accessible.

SCIENCE AND GOD

In debates about the existence of God, the findings and the claims of science usually feature prominently. For that reason, the series focuses substantially, though not exclusively, on scientific evidence.

In bringing science to the screen, The God Question series is fundamentally asking where its evidence points in relation to the existence of God.

Science has high prestige in our world. We benefit from its progress every day of our lives. In the main, science is accepted as a reliable way of gaining certain kinds of insight about our universe and the world in which we live.

Nevertheless, we must also realise that science is not – what one of our neutral contributors describes as – 'the royal road to truth'. This is a crucially important factor to recognise especially when, in debates about the existence of God, science might be presented as the only way to establish reliable information. There are many questions which science is unable to answer. Other forms of evidence are also important. This point should be borne in mind by the group during discussion.

BEWARE "GOD OF THE GAPS"

When some theists become aware of gaps in scientific knowledge, they are prone to argue that here is evidence that 'God did it'. Consequently God becomes associated with those phenomena which science presently cannot explain.

As scientific understanding progresses, the gaps systematically reduce. If they all one day disappear, there remains no need for God at all if his existence has been argued on the basis of those gaps.

Consequently many theists argue by contrast that evidence for God's existence derives from the wonders of what we do know. He is not God of the gaps.

9

LEARNING THROUGH DISCUSSION

"Exploring The God Question" is a **learning opportunity**.

Around two and a half thousand years ago, the Greek philosopher, Socrates, famously demonstrated the power of learning through discussion, dialogue and questions designed to engage the learners. This series takes that approach. The purpose is not to teach pre-conceived content and lead group members passively towards a given conclusion. Rather, it is to present them with the opportunity to consider evidence relevant to God's existence and to evaluate it for themselves.

Although it is group discussion that is envisaged, group consensus is not the object of the exercise. The aim is that individuals should develop their own views based on evidence and reason.

Group members might sometimes require additional reflective time in order to think through a question. A useful pattern might be to ask a leading question, invite some initial responses to stimulate thinking further and then give group members some time on their own to jot down their thoughts. There can then be further discussion.

It is often easier to state a belief than to argue for it. Giving reasons for beliefs might be quite challenging for some. Supplementary questions such as "Why do you think so?" and "Are you sure it couldn't be otherwise?" are often useful in encouraging people not just to express views but to explain the reasons for holding them.

Sometimes being a group leader involves initiating, encouraging, cajoling. But sometimes the role involves an element of 'crowd control': some group members might be rather boisterous or dominating. It might be necessary to respond along the lines: "Very interesting point but it would be good to hear from some others".

Disagreement is often part of the character of discussion and ought to have no connection to personal criticism. Group members – especially if they are unused to discussion – might feel somewhat uncomfortable if someone disagrees with their point of view. The group leader should encourage members to be comfortable with a level of disagreement in the group and be respectful of others who hold a different point of view from their own.

At the conclusion of the discussion, it might be helpful to summarise key points of agreement or disagreement. Perhaps these could be noted for follow up in the context of later programmes. A group member could be invited to assist in this task.

WORDS, MEANING AND THE GOD QUESTION

Sometimes arguments about God's existence produce more heat than light because participants do not have a shared understanding of the meanings of key terms. This applies to some very important words which feature frequently in the debate:

- God

- Science

- Fact

- Faith

to be the author of all natural processes which bring coherence and order to the universe; the originator of the laws which ultimately produced all life including sophisticated human beings. This is not a God easily replaced by scientific explanation; rather, he is the reason anything exists and works. For many, including atheists, this is a very different and new concept of God and much more challenging to those who claim that belief in a creator is intellectually weak and unsustainable.

1. GOD: A CREATOR OF NATURAL PROCESSES OR A COSMIC MAGICIAN?

There is a stereotype which presents God as a fantasy figure in the sky who spontaneously brings entities into existence with finger snapping ease. But science has revealed underlying processes which help us understand how many natural phenomena have developed or evolved over long periods of time. This is clearly at odds with the view that all things have been brought fully into existence with a divine finger snap. Science is quick to dismiss such a 'cosmic magician'.

Consider how the landscape of understanding and argument changes however if, rather than a 'cosmic magician', God is perceived

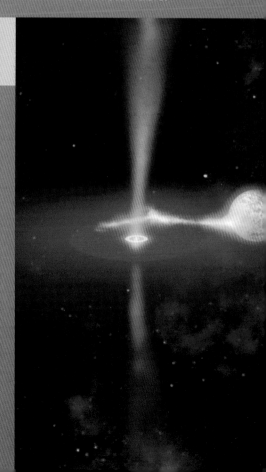

2. SCIENCE: SUGGESTING CHANCE OR INTENTION?

The issue with the word 'science' is not so much that we misunderstand its meaning, but more that there is a tendency on the part of some to exaggerate how much it can explain.

Science is a crucially important form of investigation but it should be clear that much of science is a journey of discovery. Science did not invent the universe or the laws of nature; it is not science which has produced the amazing wonders of life and the natural world. It merely seeks to understand them.

Science is discovering more and more of the astonishing mechanisms which uphold our existence and which are often so intricate and complex that scientists take centuries to comprehend them. In reality, the whole universe and world in which we live are so great that the best minds struggle to try to understand, even in part.

There is one thing on which atheists and theists regularly agree; nature looks as though it was designed for a purpose. That is, the very coherence, organisation and success of nature gives at least the appearance of design and intention.

So what is science really discovering? Might it be the processes underlying the creator's grand intention?

A common claim of atheism is that science – especially Darwinism – has shown us that there is no actual design present. But this is precisely what science cannot show. It can demonstrate order and wonder; it cannot ultimately explain it. And so we are left with the need to interpret the evidence for ourselves as we try to answer the ultimate question: are we the result of chance or intention?

That is the stark choice. Arguably, both answers are awesome in their implications. And there seems no third option. Science cannot give the answer; it can only provide evidence.

3. FACT: NOT TO BE CONFUSED WITH OPINION

It is crucially important, especially when discussing the God question, that fact and opinion do not become confused. In essence, science deals with demonstrable fact but sometimes a scientist's opinion on the God question becomes intertwined with scientific information in such a way that opinion is mistaken for fact. It is a scientific fact that the natural world is governed by the laws of physics and chemistry. To state, or suggest, that these laws do not require a creator is opinion, not fact.

One high profile television presenter, in a programme on the wonders of life, stated that it is difficult for us to accept that, at the end of our lives, there is nothing. It is impossible for him to know that. Yet because the statement is in the context of presenting scientific information, the presenter's opinion can easily sound as if it comes with scientific authority. Another, explaining how patterns in nature emerge from the laws of physics, goes on to assert that "it is tempting to think that such grand designs require a designer. Not so," he claims. But he has fallen into the trap of presenting his own opinion as a scientific conclusion. In reality, the view that such apparent design does require an initiating designer is just as logical. Both points of view are inferences or opinions and neither of them should masquerade as fact. Opinions are fundamentally important but they should be acknowledged as such.

4. THIS FAITH OR THAT: NOT A CHOICE BETWEEN SENSE AND NON-SENSE

Atheists frequently assume that having faith in God is believing without evidence. For them that is often the definition of faith. They claim that, as soon as there is evidence, there is no need for faith. They argue as follows:

- Believing in God involves faith
- Faith means believing without evidence
- There is, therefore, no evidence for believing in God

Consequently, faith in God is frequently portrayed as an intellectually barren substitute for understanding. Faith is for theists; atheists have no need of it.

Yet faith is integral to all of human life.

Typically, when asked to present evidence on which their faith in God is grounded, theists will point to the coherence and intelligibility of the universe, the astonishing complexity of each living cell and the DNA information that is at the heart of life itself. The theist, as a statement of faith, will see all of this as evidence of a creator's mind.

Faced with the same evidence, atheists will point to the developing scientific understanding of how processes combined in a complex maze of cause and effect to produce all the cosmic and earthly phenomena which have ultimately led to sophisticated human beings as the apex of all living things. The atheist will see all of this as evidence that nature, without forethought or intention, can produce such complexity. It is a statement of faith.

These mutually incompatible conclusions are each statements of faith. The view that faith is simply believing where there is no evidence should be emphatically resisted.

INTRODUCING THE PROGRAMMES TO THE GROUP

Leaders might opt to make some introductory comments about the series and its significance. In that context, some of the following points of information and advice should be helpful.

Evaluating evidence for the existence of God is much more than 'just another study topic'. It is fundamental to human lives. Therefore, in introducing the programmes to the group, the significance of the subject should be acknowledged. God's existence is fundamental to whether or not life has an overall purpose and meaning and has major implications for the decisions we make about how we choose to live.

We suggest that you should take a few minutes to draw attention to the three topics: *The Cosmos, Life and Evolution* and *Mind and Consciousness*. Group members should benefit from your guiding them to see that, over the course of the three programmes, we move from the vastness of the universe to the intricacies of the human mind. It is a journey that evokes wonder and amazement no matter the belief position of the viewer. The very success of 'nature' demands an explanation.

However, before viewing the programme with the group, it would be useful to ask what experience or interest they have in the subject. Useful prompts for this are given for each programme.

This series – with its discussion opportunities – is more than an invitation to express views. It presents important information, much of it coming from contemporary science. For viewers not used to engaging with scientific ideas, there can be some challenges involved. The group should be encouraged not to be daunted by the prospect of there being information that they don't fully grasp. It is more important to get the big picture. It is that we live in a universe of wonder that leads us to ask the fundamental question why we are here. Essentially, there are two possible answers: it all exists by chance or it exists by intention.

Like politics, 'God' is a subject that raises passions. Some members might have a strong distaste for organised religion and/or religious people; others might have a deep seated – even blind – emotional attachment to the faith of their childhood. Yet others might carry resentment about difficulties/tragedies in their lives that makes it difficult even to consider the possibility of a God. Some members might be accustomed to debating the God question and be tempted to respond to the programmes with their practised range of arguments. Whatever the preconceptions viewers carry, they should be encouraged to recognise we all have them and try to approach the programmes as openly and as honestly as possible while listening carefully to the arguments.

The God Question series attempts to present both sides of the argument. It does so on the assumption that there is less value in hearing only from those who support one's preconceived ideas. Viewers are likely to encounter challenge to their points of view. We suggest that group leaders should point out the value of listening to contrary points of view. It is, after all, only by examining the strength and weaknesses of all the arguments presented that real confidence can be built – or opinions changed!

INTRODUCING THE DVDS TO THE GROUP
Choice of Timeframes

6 Sessions	7 Sessions	12 Sessions
The programmes have been designed to be used over six sessions with each of the three topics divided into two parts. In each case there is a viewing time of around 30 minutes. (Parts 1 and 2 of programme 2 are slightly longer.)	Yet another option is to meet in session one only to introduce the ideas, the resources and the people and have a general discussion on their views of the God Question. The six sessions following would then be based on the six parts of the series, making a total of seven sessions.	Some groups might devote two sessions to each of the six half hour programmes. The first of the two might be used to view the programme followed by general discussion. The second session could then address the questions for more indepth discussion.

It is for each group to decide what suits them best. However you decide to organise the study sessions, we hope that the time given to them proves informative and rewarding.

PROGRAMME STRUCTURE AND CONTENT

Each programme can be viewed seamlessly from beginning to end but is also structured in clear sections.

The menu on the DVD can be used to revisit any of the specific sections. This means for example that if, during discussion, it seems beneficial to revisit a part of a programme, it can be easily identified and replayed using the menu.

At the end of part 1 of each programme, there is a short summary:
"The story so far... "

This is followed by a short preview of the content of upcoming part 2.

Part 2 of each programme begins with a brief review of the content of part 1.

PROMOTIONAL TRAILERS

Each DVD contains a programme (parts 1 and 2) and two promotional trailers. The first trailer provides a taster of the whole series in less than 60 seconds! The second gives a flavour of the specific programme in around two minutes. These trailers can be used to promote and advertise the sessions.

COLOUR CODED POINTERS: THE MAIN IDEAS

To enable group members to follow the narrative as clearly as possible, the Study Guide contains a running order of the key issues arising in each half hour programme. Each issue has an associated coloured dot on the page and corresponds to an on-screen coloured indicator linking what is in the Guide to what is on the screen. This enables the viewer unambiguously to know which of the issues listed on the page is being addressed in the programme at any given time.

COLOUR CODED POINTERS: NAME CAPTIONS

We believe that it will be helpful for viewers to know from the outset where key contributors stand on the fundamental issue of the series.

When contributors to The God Question are introduced, their names and biographical information appear on a band which is coloured purple or green or white. These colours are used to indicate the overall position taken by that contributor on the existence of God.

Those who argue strongly – and who are often publicly known for their position – that the evidence appears to support God's existence are associated with a purple band.

Those who argue strongly – and whose views are widely known – that the evidence does not appear to support God's existence are associated with a green band.

All others are associated with a white band.

It should not, however, be assumed that people with a white band have no view on God's existence. The white band simply indicates they have been invited to contribute specialist scientific information and their views on The God Question have not been specifically requested. In many cases, the viewer might, nevertheless, be able to infer the contributor's position on God's existence.

We request that discussion group leaders point out the colour coding before the group begins viewing.

INTRODUCING THE STUDY GUIDE TO THE GROUP

The Study Guide has been designed to be straight forward and user friendly. After a short introduction to the series, there are six sections – one for each half hour programme. It will be helpful for leaders to point out that the structure of each section of the Study Guide is as follows.

• What is at stake in this series
• A short introduction to the topic
• A colour-coded content guide to the narrative
• The big issues
• Questions for in-depth discussion
• A summary of the *case for theism* and the *case for atheism*
• Appendices including 'Understanding the Terms'
• Useful weblinks and a reading list

INTRODUCING THE QUESTIONS TO THE GROUP

There are four categories of questions for use with the group:

1. Those that invite opinion-sharing before viewing
2. General post-viewing reactions
3. Big issues questions
4. Questions for more in-depth discussion

1 QUESTIONS BEFORE VIEWING

Even before viewing the programme, it is often helpful to spend a few moments finding out what experience or knowledge group members have of the subject. Questions are offered in the Leader's Manual for each programme under the heading "Preparing for Viewing".

2 POST VIEWING REACTION

After viewing, questions are key to a successful discussion.

Experience suggests that very general questions such as 'What was your reaction to the programme?' provide a good starting point. For each programme, the Leader's Manual provides such broad questions under the heading "Inviting Initial Reactions". These questions can be used many times in the course of viewing and discussing the series.

3 QUESTIONS ON BIG ISSUES

Following discussion of overall reaction to the programme, there are three or four questions labelled "The Big Issues". These big issues questions are reproduced in the Study Guide also.

4 QUESTIONS FOR MORE IN-DEPTH DISCUSSION

Finally, there are questions specific to key themes in the programmes. These are found only in the Study Guide.

A FLEXIBLE APPROACH

All the questions are designed in some way to be thought provoking and to stimulate engaged discussion. That is their sole purpose. At any point in the process, the discussion might 'take off'. In this case, the questions might become less important. It is quality discussion which counts, however it arises.

Where group members are comfortable with free-flowing discussion, the leader might focus attention on the Big Issues questions with less reference to the in-depth discussion questions.

Another option would be for leaders to ignore the Big Issues questions and go straight to the in-depth questions. All of these options might be discussed with the group.

The questions for in-depth discussion are designed to help the group engage with key aspects of the programme. Nevertheless, leaders are still encouraged to be selective and should not see the omission of certain questions as a failure to complete the task.

The in-depth questions are introduced using quotations from contributors. In many cases, these represent conflicting points of view which are at the heart of the debate. Leaders should quite frequently draw the group's attention to these quotations. They should prove an important background for thinking through the associated question. As group participants express their own views, it might often be useful to ask how they would respond to any of the quotations which provide a contrary view.

AND FINALLY...

Good questions are generally 'open' questions: they don't invite the answer 'yes' or 'no'.

In many cases, the questions for group discussion might appear to be 'closed' questions. The explanation is that often 'open' questions can appear more complex and more like an exam challenge. For that reason, questions have sometimes been asked in a very straightforward way such as "Do you agree that....?" The alternative "To what extent do you agree that...?" is more open but sounds more convoluted and exam linked. However, we suggest group leaders might often wish to turn apparently closed questions into open questions by adding for example, "Why do you think so?" We have tried to avoid the monotony of constantly including the supplementary 'why do you think so?' in print but it is an important aspect of developing discussion.

Programme 1 :
EXPLORING THE GOD QUESTION —
THE COSMOS (PART 1)

WHAT IS AT STAKE IN THIS PROGRAMME...

...is whether scientific discoveries about the birth and development of our universe suggest that a creator is essential to its success — or as dispensable as the mythological gods of ancient Greece and Rome.

INTRODUCING THE COSMOS

(This introduction is reproduced in the Study Guide)

Debating the existence of God leads us to face ultimate questions. Chief among them is the issue of where we came from. This programme explores what orthodox science believes about 'the beginning' and what happened next!

The belief that our universe came from the 'big bang' is well known and widely accepted. Often less appreciated, is that the 'big bang' resulted in order not chaos! That order was produced through a sequence of spectacular events that scientists believe led eventually to life being birthed on planet earth.

As these mysteries have been explored, there have been major advances in knowledge and understanding.   However, important underlying questions remain — such as:

'Is science making God unnecessary or discovering the work of a creator?'

'Does the order in the universe provide evidence of God or not?'

These questions are not within the scope of science to answer - yet it does provide crucial evidence.

In the 21st century, the subject of God's existence remains a 'hot topic'. This programme highlights the prominent ongoing debate between atheists and theists and, through investigating the wonders of the cosmos, asks if what we are learning through science appears to reduce the case for God's existence or, instead, supports it.

GENERAL AIMS

- To recognise the importance of the debate about God and science and to be encouraged to participate in it.

- To examine the view that discovering scientific explanations about our world and the universe beyond removes the need for a creator.

- To understand the arguments on both sides of the debate about evidence for the existence of God.

AIMS FOR PART 1

- To set the current debate about God's existence in its modern and historical context.

- To learn about various forms of order that came from the Big Bang, believed to have brought our universe into existence.

- To discuss whether the scientific information about the birth and development of the cosmos points to it being the product of chance events or the mind of a creator.

SYNOPSIS – A LEADER'S GUIDE TO THE NARRATIVE

(There is a separate content guide in the Study Guide for the use of group members during viewing.)

- A very public debate is taking place between atheists and theists about evidence for the existence of God. Science has become an important battleground.

- Today, the movement known as New Atheism frequently presents scientific knowledge and understanding as a reason to dispense with God.

- Historically, there have been some key figures contributing to the view that science and religion are in conflict - notably Galileo and Darwin. In the case of Galileo, the real story seems to have been rather different from how it is often told. It was a dispute about whether Aristotle or Galileo was scientifically correct; it was not a conflict about science and God.

- In ancient Greece, the emergence of science eroded belief in their gods; yet belief in the God of the Bible not only survived the birth of modern science but, some argue, led to the birth of the scientific revolution in the 16th century.

- The God question is whether or not this God remains compatible with what 21st century science reveals about the universe.

- Scientific knowledge about the origin and early development of the cosmos has unravelled an amazing story of how order began to emerge in it. It also raises many fundamental questions - about how and why.

Programme 1 :

EXPLORING THE GOD QUESTION - THE COSMOS (PART 1)

PREPARING FOR VIEWING

Before viewing, group members might wish to share briefly their own initial thoughts on the God question. In the group, what is the balance of agnostics/atheists/believers in God? What is the common opinion among friends, work colleagues and family about the existence of God?

Consider if there are points of information from the introduction to the Leader's Manual that should be shared or reinforced at this point.

VIEWING THE PROGRAMME

Group members might wish to use the programme content guide in their booklet while viewing.

SEPARATING FACT FROM OPINION

While viewing the programmes and addressing the discussion questions it will be useful to distinguish between:

- statements of fact
- interpretation of facts
- opinion based more on intuition than evidence

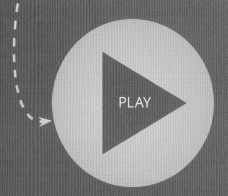

PLAY

TER VIEWING THE PROGRAMME

It might be helpful to remind the group that Part 1 of the programme:

- Began by introducing the ongoing debate between theists and atheists about science and religion
- It then reviewed the famous clash between Galileo and the church of his time
- Thereafter, the programme recounted how the ancient mythological gods withered away in the light of scientific thinking but the God of the Bible remains
- Next, the documentary presented the findings of contemporary science about the origin and early development of the universe and asked: is there space for this God in the age of scientific discovery?

INITIAL REACTIONS

(These questions are not in the Study Guide, but you may choose to consider them.)

1 What is your overall initial reaction to the programme?

2 What aspect of the programme stood out for you – for example, was there some important new information? Or did something confirm or alter your view on the God question?
Was there a statement that you found enlightening – or even infuriating?

3 Consider the view that you currently have about whether or not God exists. Did you find your view seriously challenged by contributors to the programme who have a different opinion?

THE BIG ISSUES

(reproduced in Study Guide)

 WHY DO **SCIENCE AND RELIGION** APPEAR, TO SOME, TO BE IN **CONFLICT?**
WHAT CONTRIBUTION HAS BEEN MADE BY NEW ATHEISTS SUCH AS **RICHARD DAWKINS**, AUTHOR OF 'THE GOD DELUSION'?

 DO THE CONCLUSIONS OF **CONTEMPORARY SCIENCE** ABOUT THE ORIGIN AND **DEVELOPMENT OF THE UNIVERSE** LEND SUPPORT TO BELIEF IN **GOD'S EXISTENCE** OR UNDERMINE IT?

 ACCORDING TO PETER ATKINS, THE EXISTENCE OF GOD IS **"ONE OF THE BIGGEST QUESTIONS OF ALL".**
DO YOU AGREE?

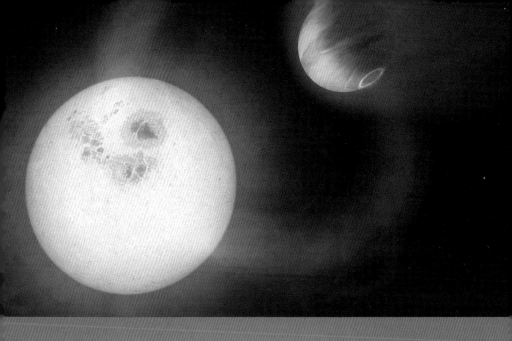

QUESTIONS FOR MORE
IN-DEPTH DISCUSSION

Follow Questions 1–8 in the Study Guide

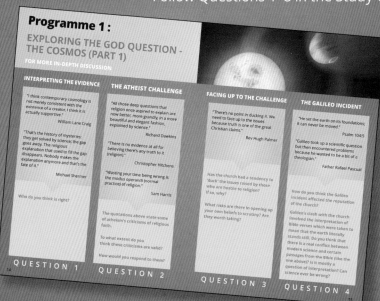

Programme 1 :

EXPLORING THE GOD QUESTION - THE COSMOS (PART 1)

FOR MORE IN-DEPTH DISCUSSION

INTERPRETING THE EVIDENCE

"I think contemporary cosmology is not merely consistent with the existence of a creator, I think it is actually supportive."

William Lane Craig

"That's the history of mysteries: they get solved by science; the gap goes away. The religious explanation that used to fill the gap disappears. Nobody makes the explanation anymore and that's the fate of it."

Michael Shermer

Who do you think is right?

QUESTION 1

14

THE ATHEIST CHALLENGE

"All those deep questions that religion once aspired to explain are now better, more grandly, in a more beautiful and elegant fashion, explained by science."

Richard Dawkins

"There is no evidence at all for believing there's any truth to it (religion)."

Christopher Hitchens

"Wasting your time being wrong is the modus operandi (normal practice) of religion."

Sam Harris

The quotations above state some of atheism's criticisms of religious faith.

To what extent do you think these criticisms are valid?

How would you respond to them?

QUESTION 2

FACING UP TO THE CHALLENGE

"There's no point in ducking it. We need to face up to the issues because truth is one of the great Christian claims."

Rev Hugh Palmer

Has the church had a tendency to 'duck' the issues raised by those who are hostile to religion? If so, why?

What risks are there in opening up your own beliefs to scrutiny? Are they worth taking?

QUESTION 3

THE GALILEO INCIDENT

"He set the earth on its foundations; it can never be moved."

Psalm 104:5

"Galileo took up a scientific question but then encountered problems because he wanted to be a bit of a theologian."

Father Rafael Pascual

How do you think the Galileo incident affected the reputation of the church?

Galileo's clash with the church involved the interpretation of Bible verses which were taken to mean that the earth literally stands still. Do you think that there is a real conflict between modern science and certain passages from the Bible (like the one above)? Is it mostly a question of interpretation? Can science ever be wrong?

QUESTION 4

15

Programme 1 :
EXPLORING THE GOD QUESTION –
THE COSMOS (PART 2)

WHAT IS AT STAKE IN THIS PROGRAMME...

...IS WHETHER SCIENTIFIC DISCOVERIES ABOUT THE BIRTH AND DEVELOPMENT OF OUR UNIVERSE SUGGEST THAT A CREATOR IS ESSENTIAL TO ITS SUCCESS - OR AS DISPENSABLE AS THE MYTHOLOGICAL GODS OF ANCIENT GREECE AND ROME.

SPECIFICALLY IN PART 2...

Is our universe, with all its precision necessary to support life, more likely to be the result of chance or the work of a creator?

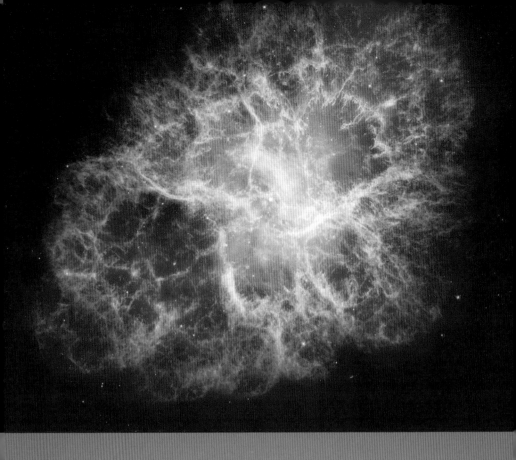

AIMS FOR PART 2

- To reflect on whether the Bible's account of the creation of the universe runs counter to the view of modern science about the birth and development of the universe.

- To consider if the question "Who made God?" successfully undermines the case for a creator.

- To consider if the multiverse idea removes the need for a creator.

- To learn about the extent of fine-tuning necessary in the universe for life to exist on earth.

- To assess whether the scientific information about the laws and fine-tuning of the universe for life on earth, point to a series of chance events or the mind of a creator.

- To draw a conclusion about the extent to which our knowledge and understanding of order in the cosmos makes a contribution to answering the God question.

SYNOPSIS – A LEADER'S GUIDE TO THE NARRATIVE

(There is a separate content guide in the Study Guide for the use of group members during viewing.)

- Although some might conclude that the universe shows signs of a creator, atheists highlight a number of issues that, to them, point in the opposite direction. This includes speculating that much of the universe might be 'a waste of stuff'.

- Theists challenge this on scientific grounds and point out that there is still the fundamental question of how a universe could have emerged without some 'transcendent cause.' Atheists respond with the question 'who made God?' Theists counter that this is a nonsensical question.

- There is the further question for believers: how to interpret Genesis. Does it describe six literal days of 'hectic divine activity' or should it be further interpreted in the light of modern scientific information?

- Atheists accept that if there is no creator, then a major challenge for science is to discover how otherwise a universe could come into existence. Could our universe have been created out of 'nothing'? This hypothesis is considered with reference to a concept known as "the multiverse".

- One thing is certain: life is dependent on the consistency of a set of laws in the universe as well as their astonishing precision and fine tuning. So much so that they can be described in a special language: mathematics. Theists and atheists dispute whether the fine tuning can be convincingly explained using the multiverse concept.

- Theists and atheists deliver their concluding statements*.

---

* A summary of 'The Case for Theism' and 'The Case for Atheism' is provided as an Appendix within the Study Guide at the end of Part 2 of The Cosmos.

Programme 1 :

EXPLORING THE GOD QUESTION - THE COSMOS (PART 2)

PREPARING FOR VIEWING

Remind the group that Part 1 of the programme:

- Introduced the ongoing debate between theists and atheists about science and religion and then reviewed the Galileo incident

- Next, the documentary presented the findings of contemporary science about the origin and early development of the universe.

If time permits, re-cap on some of the key points, issues or controversies arising from the previous session.

VIEWING THE PROGRAMME

Group members might wish to use the programme content guide in their booklet while viewing.

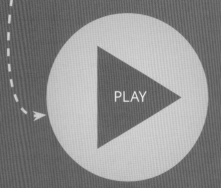

PLAY

FTER VIEWING THE PROGRAMME

As a reminder, Part 2:

- Began by atheists challenging the evidence for a universe created by God

- There was then the further issue of a possible clash between the Genesis account and the scientific account of the origin of the universe

- In building a case for atheism, it was accepted that there has to be some scientific explanation for the origin of the universe which attempts to be completely independent of the involvement of a creator. The programme investigated the possibility of a multiverse – that our universe could have originated as one of many millions of embryonic universes which theoretically might 'pop' into existence

- Finally, the programme demonstrated that, whatever its origin, our universe is truly remarkable. It is a place of order governed by finely tuned forces which make life possible. These observations raise the issue why the universe should be like this and pose the question: is this evidence of a creator?

INITIAL REACTIONS

1 What is your overall initial reaction to the programme?

2 What aspect of the programme stood out for you – for example, was there some important new information? Or did something confirm or alter your view on the God question?
Was there a statement that you found enlightening – or even infuriating?

3 Consider the view that you currently have about whether or not God exists. Did you find your view seriously challenged by contributors to the programme who have a different opinion?

THE BIG ISSUES

(reproduced in Study Guide)

? THE **UNIVERSE** APPEARS TO BE **FINE TUNED FOR LIFE**. IS THIS A CONVINCING ARGUMENT FOR THE **EXISTENCE OF GOD?**

? DOES THE **MULTIVERSE CONCEPT** UNDERMINE **THE CASE FOR GOD?**

? CAN THE **BIBLICAL CREATION STORY** SQUARE WITH OUR CURRENT UNDERSTANDING OF **COSMOLOGY?**

QUESTIONS FOR MORE IN-DEPTH DISCUSSION

Follow Questions 1–5 in the Study Guide

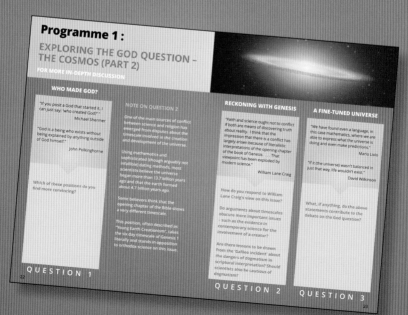

Programme 1 :

EXPLORING THE GOD QUESTION – THE COSMOS (PART 2)

FOR MORE IN-DEPTH DISCUSSION

WHO MADE GOD?

"If you posit a God that started it, I can just say: 'who created God?'."
Michael Shermer

"God is a being who exists without being explained by anything outside of God himself."
John Polkinghorne

Which of these positions do you find more convincing?

QUESTION 1

22

NOTE ON QUESTION 2

One of the main sources of conflict between science and religion has emerged from disputes about the timescale involved in the creation and development of the universe.

Using mathematics and sophisticated (though arguably not infallible) dating methods, most scientists believe the universe began more than 13.7 billion years ago and that the earth formed about 4.7 billion years ago.

Some believers think that the opening chapter of the Bible shows a very different timescale.

This position, often described as "Young Earth Creationism", takes the six day timescale of Genesis 1 literally and stands in opposition to orthodox science on this issue.

RECKONING WITH GENESIS

"Faith and science ought not to conflict if both are means of discovering truth about reality. I think that the impression that there is a conflict has largely arisen because of literalistic interpretations of the opening chapter of the book of Genesis . . . That viewpoint has been exploded by modern science."
William Lane Craig

How do you respond to William Lane Craig's view on this issue?

Do arguments about timescales obscure more important issues - such as the evidence in contemporary science for the involvement of a creator?

Are there lessons to be drawn from the 'Galileo incident' about the dangers of dogmatism in scriptural interpretation? Should scientists also be cautious of dogmatism?

QUESTION 2

23

A FINE-TUNED UNIVERSE

"We have found even a language, in this case mathematics, where we are able to express what the universe is doing and even make predictions."
Mario Livio

"If it (the universe) wasn't balanced in just that way, life wouldn't exist."
David Wilkinson

What, if anything, do the above statements contribute to the debate on the God question?

QUESTION 3

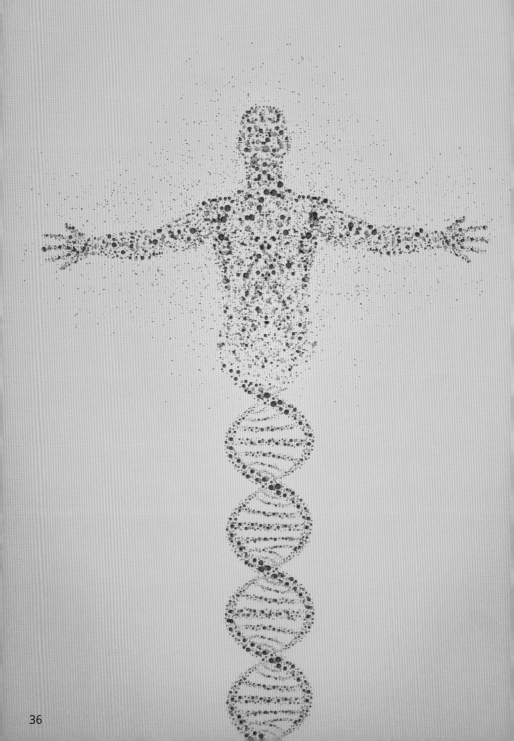

Programme 2 :
EXPLORING THE GOD QUESTION - LIFE AND EVOLUTION (PART 1)

WHAT IS AT STAKE IN THIS PROGRAMME...

...is whether or not it is justifiable to claim that unguided evolutionary forces, without the involvement of a creator are, in themselves, powerful enough to have produced all of the sophisticated life forms that have ever existed, including human beings.

INTRODUCING LIFE & EVOLUTION

(This introduction is reproduced in the Study Guide)

Programme 1 investigated some of the wonders of the origin and development of the cosmos. Now we focus on a most astonishing characteristic of our universe: life on earth.

In orthodox science, understanding the development of life is rooted in the work of Charles Darwin and his theory of evolution. Since the publication of Darwin's "On the Origin of Species" in 1859, atheists have seized on Darwin's work in their effort to dispense with God. Consequently, millions across the world live on the assumption that they must choose between evolution and belief in a creator. They include many in the Christian church who see no possible means of reconciling evolution with the Genesis account of creation. The same issue arises in Islam.

But even if evolution is eventually rejected, on theological and/or scientific grounds, first it should be understood.

Part 1 of the programme explains and illustrates the basic principles that evolutionists believe are operating in the natural world. Atheists argue that this understanding allows them to dispense with God.
But the programme also introduces well respected eminent evolutionary scientists who are also people of faith. They argue that evolution succeeds because it is the work of a creator who wanted it to be so. This suggests that it is not the science that opposes God but rather how atheists interpret it.

Nevertheless, other scientists, many of them within the Christian community, are sceptical about fundamental aspects of Darwinism. Their perspective is also presented.

Some objections to evolution are more theological than scientific. In that regard, Part 2 includes some debate about the interpretation of the opening chapters of Genesis.

The ongoing debate about our origins, evolution, the Bible and God is fundamentally important. This programme aims to help viewers to understand it better and to identify for themselves where they stand on these highly significant issues.

Regardless of which scientific theories most accurately describe the development of life on earth, arguably the most important question is whether its very success seems ultimately to be the work of a creator or the product of chance and good fortune.

THE KEY PURPOSES OF THIS PROGRAMME

Evolution and God is a topic that often causes strong feelings and deep division. That is clearly evidenced in the programme. The purpose of this programme is neither to defend evolution nor to attack it. Rather it is, first of all, to understand its basic principles and the associated evidence.

Secondly, it is to examine if evolution – even if entirely accepted – poses a serious threat to God.

Thirdly, it is to investigate possible tension points between theism and evolution.

GENERAL AIMS

- To recognise the role and impact of Darwinism in the wider debate about the existence of God.

- To assess the extent to which the theory of evolution presents a significant challenge to belief in the existence of God or, instead, supports the case for God.

AIMS FOR PART 1

- To understand the basic insights and conclusions of Charles Darwin in relation to his theory of evolution.

- To recognise the central importance of the theory of evolution to an atheistic worldview.

- To realise that many significant scientists reconcile evolution and a belief in God.

- To highlight the ideological impact, beginning in the mid nineteenth century, of Darwinism on religious belief.

- To reflect on what the science of genetics, together with the fossil record, contribute to an understanding of Darwin's theory but also to consider how it might provide evidence for God.

- To query the adequacy of the explanation offered by natural selection.

- To consider the view that there is direct evidence of 'Intelligent Design'.

In preparation for viewing the programme, group members can be made aware of the following basic viewpoints (reproduced in Study Guide) on evolution and God. It is likely that group members themselves will take one of the four positions noted below. Opinions might be strongly held so leaders should emphasise the challenge but also the rewards of listening openly to other points of view.

FOUR DISTINCT PERSPECTIVES ON EVOLUTION

INTRODUCTION

Increasingly, since the publication of Darwin's "On the Origin of Species" in 1859, evolution has become the dominating idea in life sciences. Atheists present evolution as the scientific alternative to God. However, many theists (highly prominent scientists among them) embrace evolution – seeing it as God's method of creation – and object to it being offered as an alternative to God. Other theists have different levels of difficulty with evolution and some reject it altogether.

ATHEISTIC EVOLUTION

Atheists argue that, over billions of years - and with no need for a creator at any stage - the blind forces of natural selection have produced all the variety of species that have ever existed. Sophisticated human beings also emerged from that process. The origin of all life is derived from the first living cell. God is unnecessary because the whole process is capable of developing by itself. However most admit that it is not yet known how life began.

THEISTIC EVOLUTION

Theistic evolutionists agree with the orthodox scientific explanation for the development of life. That is, natural forces are sufficient to create all the diversity and sophistication that we see but that this has resulted from the potential built into the universe by God at the first moments of creation. Theistic evolutionists generally take the view that God sustains the laws of the universe and holds the whole system in place. For them, evolution by natural selection operates within that broad framework and is largely responsible for all the diversity and sophistication in the natural world. Through evolution, God has given nature freedom with potential. All evolutionists accept that the processes took place over vast periods of time, estimated to be around four billion years of time on earth.

INTELLIGENT DESIGN

Intelligent Design proponents hold that certain identifiable features of the natural world and of living things are best explained by an intelligent cause rather than an undirected process such as natural selection. There are many immensely complex biological phenomena that are too sophisticated to have evolved through a series of chance mutations. The complexities of just one single living cell is a prime example. The wonder of the human genome built by the language of DNA is another. This information is like an instruction book for how every living thing is constructed. The inference is that this is evidence of a designing mind at work. Some intelligent design proponents accept that evolutionary forces operate in the world but that they are far from being the whole story.

YOUNG EARTH CREATIONISM

Young Earth Creationists claim that the earth is of much more recent origin (usually less than 10,000 years) and that God created the universe, the world and all original life forms including human beings in six twenty-four hour days. This view is rooted in the belief that the early chapters of Genesis in the Bible must be interpreted literally. Such timescales are far too short for evolution to work. The implication therefore is that evolutionary scientists are mistaken in their interpretation of the evidence.

SYNOPSIS – A LEADER'S GUIDE TO THE NARRATIVE

(There is a separate content guide in the Study Guide for the use of group members during viewing.)

- There is no more controversial a figure in the science religion debate than Charles Darwin. He has been adopted as a cornerstone of atheism. Many scientists view Darwinian evolution as a satisfactory alternative to a creator.

- Significant numbers of believers see evolution as irreconcilable with God and so reject it. However, there are many, scientists among them, who believe there is no conflict between evolution and belief in God.

- Although there was general acceptance of Darwin's ideas in the religious community of his day, his work nevertheless ignited a controversy which continues today.

- The central idea in Darwin's work is 'evolution by natural selection'. He observed that creatures develop variations - some of which become crucial to survival. Those which survive appear to have been 'selected' by nature.

- In Darwinian evolution, over vast periods of time, an accumulation of small changes is believed to produce the variety of species we find in all of life on earth.

- The fossil record, found in the world's rocks, appears to lend support to Darwin's idea of gradual development over time. Whether they believe in God or not, scientists are agreed it is an astonishing story.

- Theistic evolutionists emphasise that evolution 'works' because it is God's method of creation.

- While the explanatory power of natural selection is generally accepted among scientists, there are some who find it unconvincing. Intelligent Design theorists argue that there is positive evidence for design in many specific forms of nature and that these cannot effectively be scientifically explained by evolution through natural selection alone.

- Since Darwin's time, the structure of DNA has been discovered. It reveals how an 'information system' lies at the heart of life. Some theists see evidence in this of the mind and intelligence of God while atheists argue that exclusively natural forces must be a sufficient explanation.

- Although atheists opt to have faith in the blind forces of nature, believers emphasise that, whether or not Darwin was right, the sheer wonder of the development of life inescapably points to the involvement of a creator.

Programme 2 :

EXPLORING THE GOD QUESTION - LIFE AND EVOLUTION (PART 1)

PREPARING FOR VIEWING

Before viewing, group members might wish to share their initial views/understanding of evolution. What do they think it means? Why is it so important to 'the God question'? How do friends, work colleagues etc view the subject? How common/unusual is it to accept evolution and belief in God?

Group leaders might discuss the FOUR DISTINCT PERSPECTIVES ON EVOLUTION with group members. See page 50 in Study Guide.

VIEWING THE PROGRAMME

Group members might wish to use the programme content guide in their booklet while viewing.

SEPARATING FACT FROM OPINION

While viewing the programme and addressing the discussion questions it will be useful to distinguish between:

• statements of fact

• interpretation of facts

• opinion based more on intuition than evidence

Please note that the duration of Programme 2 Part 1 (40 minutes) is longer than other parts of the series. After 25 minutes, a fade to black indicates an opportunity to pause the programme to reflect on the story so far. Any of questions 1,2,3,5 and 7 could be discussed at this point.

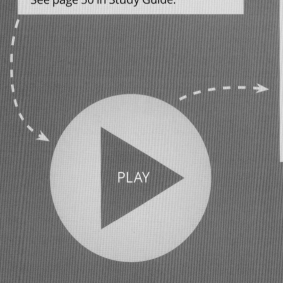

PLAY

As a reminder :

Part 1 of the programme began by introducing the work of Charles Darwin and his theory of evolution. Darwin described his chief insight as 'evolution by natural selection'. Darwin used this concept to explain how differences arise between members of the same species.

Darwin then reasoned that, over long periods of time, the differences might accumulate to such an extent that separate species emerge. But Darwin went even further and suggested that all the diversity we see in the world today could be traced back to one common source: the first spark of life. Darwin reckoned that all of life, including human beings, evolved through this process and from one original ancestor.

In summary, natural selection may be stated as follows:

- Over time and over the generations, small changes randomly occur in species
- Some of those changes may give a survival advantage to the offspring in the environment where they live
- Where that is the case, it is as if nature has 'selected' those characteristics beneficial for survival
- Those species that do not possess characteristics beneficial for survival are more likely to become extinct

This was a revolutionary view that appeared to be a very different account of the development of life from the Genesis story in the Bible where, if the text is interpreted literally, species came 'ready made'. There is some disagreement about how Darwin's ideas were received in religious circles but it seems clear that some leading theologians were entirely accepting of them.

There are at least two hugely important questions arising from Darwin's work.

The first is: was Darwin's theory of evolution by natural selection substantially correct and even, if so, how much does the theory of evolution successfully explain?

The second is: even assuming evolution is substantially correct, does this necessarily and logically remove the need for God?

Discoveries in genetics and also in the fossil record convince most scientists that Darwin's theory was well founded. The fact that the DNA of all living things shows remarkable similarities is used to argue some kind of common origin; the fossil record points to older organisms being simple and later organisms being more complex. Both of these factors appear to be consistent with evolutionary development. But why should the natural world work this way? Is natural selection an adequate and comprehensive explanation for life on earth? All theists see the manifestation of a transcendent God at some level; some see it in the details, others see it more in the big picture.

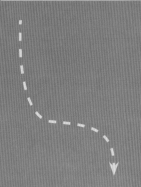

INITIAL REACTIONS

1 What is your overall initial reaction to the programme?

2 Did any aspect of the programme stand out for you – eg, was there some important new information? Or did something confirm or alter your view on the God question? Was there a statement that you found enlightening – or even infuriating?

3 Consider the view that you currently have about whether or not God exists. Did you find your view seriously challenged by contributors to the programme who have a different opinion?

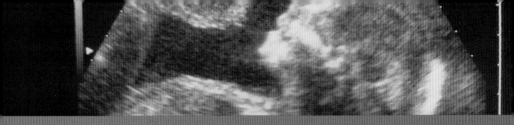

THE BIG ISSUES
(reproduced in Study Guide)

WHY DOES **EVOLUTION** APPARENTLY POSE SUCH A **THREAT TO GOD?**

BELIEF IN THE POWER OF **NATURAL SELECTION** LIES AT THE HEART OF **DARWINIAN EVOLUTION.** HOW PERSUADED ARE YOU BY DARWIN'S CENTRAL IDEA?

RICHARD DAWKINS BELIEVES THERE IS THE **"APPEARANCE OF DESIGN"** IN NATURE. WHAT DO YOU THINK HE MEANS BY 'DESIGN' AND HOW DO YOU RESPOND TO HIS ARGUMENT THAT **BLIND FORCES OF EVOLUTION** CONVINCINGLY EXPLAIN THE "APPEARANCE OF DESIGN"?

HOW RELEVANT TO THE GOD QUESTION IS THE EXISTENCE OF THE **DNA INFORMATION** THAT IS NOW KNOWN TO BE **CRUCIAL** IN THE CONSTRUCTION OF **ALL LIVING CELLS?**

QUESTIONS FOR MORE
IN-DEPTH DISCUSSION
Follow Questions 1–8 in the Study Guide

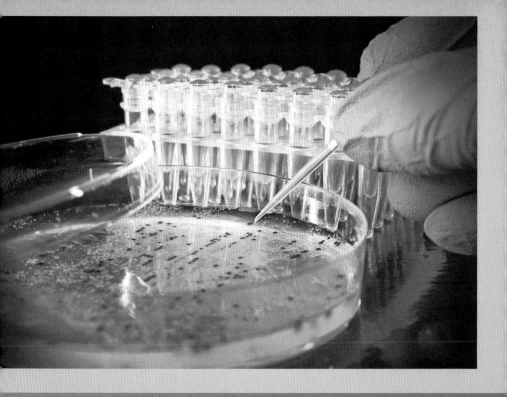

Programme 2:
EXPLORING THE GOD QUESTION - LIFE AND EVOLUTION (PART 2)

WHAT IS AT STAKE IN THIS PROGRAMME...

....IS WHETHER OR NOT IT IS JUSTIFIABLE TO CLAIM THAT UNGUIDED EVOLUTIONARY FORCES, WITHOUT ANY INVOLVEMENT OF A CREATOR ARE, IN THEMSELVES, POWERFUL ENOUGH TO HAVE PRODUCED ALL THE SOPHISTICATED LIFE FORMS THAT HAVE EVER EXISTED INCLUDING HUMAN BEINGS.

SPECIFICALLY IN PART 2...

How convincing is the evolutionary account and can it really be compatible with belief in God and reverence for Holy Scripture?

AIMS FOR PART 2

- To consider various levels of scepticism about the extent of evolution's explanatory power.

- To recognise that there are mysteries surrounding the development of life that are presently outwith the power of evolution to explain.

- To enquire about the extent to which (Bible-based) theism and the theory of evolution can be aligned.

- To draw a conclusion about whether our knowledge about the sophistication of life processes makes a contribution to answering the God question.

Evolutio

Evolution is
developmen
gradual pro
the change
a different

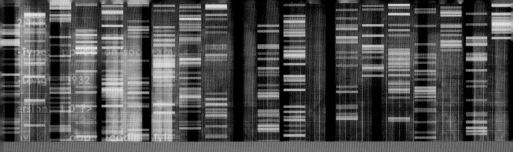

SYNOPSIS – A LEADER'S GUIDE TO THE NARRATIVE

(There is a separate content guide in the Study Guide for the use of group members during viewing.)

- Although some theists are convinced that the scientific explanation for the development of life on earth is best understood as 'evolution by natural selection', others are sceptical about how much it really explains.

- Intelligent Design theorists argue that the sophistication of the digital code at the heart of life itself is clear evidence of supernatural intelligence. They are very unconvinced that the language of DNA can be the product of random evolutionary processes.

- At the heart of this argument is whether random trial and error changes taking place over billions of years could actually have produced all the sophistication of life. Evolutionary scientists counter with the view that, given billions of years to explore the possibilities and build on their survival advantages, evolution can convincingly explain all the diversity of life.

- A further challenge to the view that Darwinian evolution is a comprehensive explanation for all of life is that evolutionary biology is, so far, unable to explain the origin of life itself.

- Life itself would never have been possible if planet earth had not provided many life fostering conditions.

- For theists who believe that evolution is a convincing scientific explanation for all the sophistication of life, there are some intriguing challenges to face. These include: understanding why a creator might have chosen such an apparently cruel and wasteful method of creation as evolution; being convinced that evolution could produce creatures in the image of God; reconciling evolution with the Genesis story and speculating about where in the process God-consciousness emerged.

- Nevertheless, one 'neutral' scientist believes he has discovered an intriguing relationship between the evolutionary story and the Genesis account of creation.

- Theists and atheists deliver their concluding statements*.

---

*A summary of 'The Case for Theism' and 'The Case for Atheism' is provided as an Appendix within the Study Guide at the end of Part 2 Life and Evolution.

Programme 2 :

EXPLORING THE GOD QUESTION - LIFE AND EVOLUTION (PART 2)

PREPARING FOR VIEWING

Remind the group that Part 1:

- ...was a basic introduction to evolution and presented some of the contemporary evidence that appears to support it.

- Scientifically and theologically, Darwinism was revolutionary; there were mixed reports evident about the reaction of the church of Darwin's time.

- Although evolution is fundamentally important to atheism, there are many – high profile scientists among them – who see evolution as the process used by the creator to achieve his purposes. They see no conflict therefore between evolution and belief in God.

- For others, it is not so straight forward and, for them, the scientific premises of evolution need to be challenged.

If time permits, re-cap on some of the key points, issues or controversies arising from the previous session.

PLAY

VIEWING THE PROGRAMME

Group members might wish to use the programme content guide in their booklet while viewing.

As a reminder, Part 2 of the programme:

- Began by recognising that what evolution attempts to explain is truly mind blowing. So much so, that some scientists remain unconvinced about how much explanatory power evolutionary theory really has. While the principle of natural selection is largely uncontroversial, some express much more doubt about the likelihood of all the complexity and diversity in our contemporary world having emerged from millions of small random changes, each of which has been 'selected' and built upon over many generations. As a blind unguided process it seems, to some, too incredible.

- Evolutionary theory states that life developed from simple to more complex forms. Although the fossil record seems to support this, the science of genetics has established that what was once believed to be simple – a single cell – is immensely intricate and complex. So was there ever a simple beginning as evolution claims? Is evolutionary theory missing something? At the cell's complex heart is DNA – an instruction manual for how to build the organism: whether it is a plant, an animal or a human being. Those instructions are not living things but are in the form of information or data and so it is difficult to see how it could evolve in the way that a living thing could. So where did the information come from? Those who see evolution as being far from the whole story question how data could evolve without being produced by an intelligent mind. Is this evidence of the mind of God?

- A further mystery for now is that there is relatively little understanding of life's origin. So there is much that is unknown. But what is already known is even more important to the theists' argument. Some theists, who are substantially convinced that evolutionary theory is correct, believe that its very success is because a creator is behind the whole process.

- The hospitable conditions of planet earth have been essential to the success of life. The 'life-friendly' environment is not within the scope of evolution to explain.

- Those who believe that evolution is God's creative plan must face up to some difficult questions before evolution and belief in God can be convincingly aligned.

- Meanwhile, atheists maintain that, although evolution has many unanswered questions, it is more sensible and credible to look only to science for ultimate explanations than to give any credence to the possibility of a creator being involved.

INITIAL REACTIONS

1 What is your overall initial reaction to the programme?

2 What aspect of the programme stood out for you – for example, was there some important new information? Or did something confirm or alter your view on the God question?
Was there a statement that you found enlightening – or even infuriating?

3 Consider the view that you currently have about whether or not God exists. Did you find your view seriously challenged by contributors to the programme who have a different opinion?

THE BIG ISSUES
(reproduced in Study Guide)

EVOLUTION DEPENDS ON **'RANDOM' CHANGES** TAKING PLACE IN **ORGANISMS**. SOME ARGUE THAT, GIVEN ENOUGH TIME, THIS IS A VIABLE WAY FOR SOPHISTICATED **LIFE TO DEVELOP**; OTHERS DISPUTE THAT.
WHAT DO YOU THINK?

DO YOU THINK THERE CAN BE ANY ACCOMMODATION BETWEEN **GENESIS 1 AND 2** AND **EVOLUTIONARY BIOLOGY?**

THE PROGRAMME RAISES SOME IMPORTANT ISSUES THAT NEED TO BE RESOLVED IF ONE WISHES TO BE A **DARWINIAN** AND A **BELIEVER IN GOD.**
THESE INCLUDE:

- WHETHER OR NOT THE SUFFERING WHICH IS APPARENTLY AN INTEGRAL PART OF THE EVOLUTIONARY PROCESS IS COMPATIBLE WITH A GOOD AND LOVING GOD;

- HOW A RANDOM 'CHANCE' PROCESS COULD BE RELIED UPON TO PRODUCE CREATURES IN THE IMAGE OF GOD.

(MORE DETAILS ARE GIVEN IN APPENDIX 3 IN THE STUDY GUIDE ON PAGE 54 OF THE STUDY GUIDE)

DO YOU THINK THESE ISSUES ARE RESOLVABLE OR IS EVOLUTION NOT CONSISTENT WITH BELIEF IN A CREATOR?

QUESTIONS FOR MORE IN-DEPTH DISCUSSION
Follow Questions 1–8 in the Study Guide

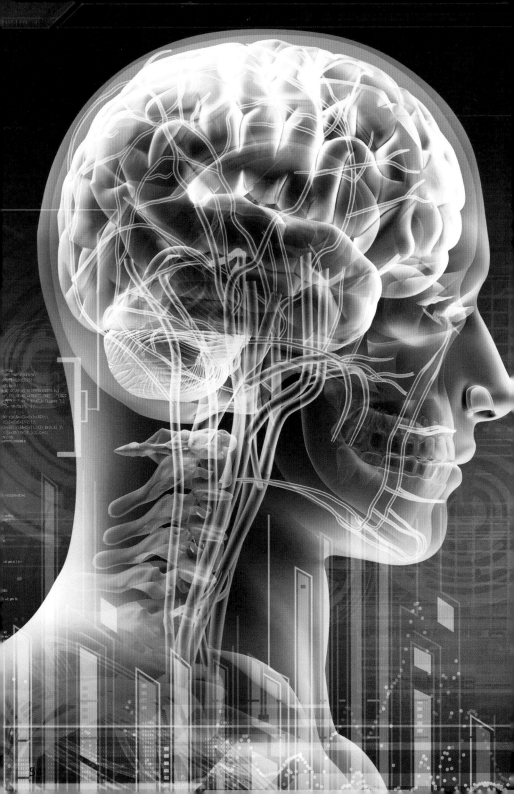

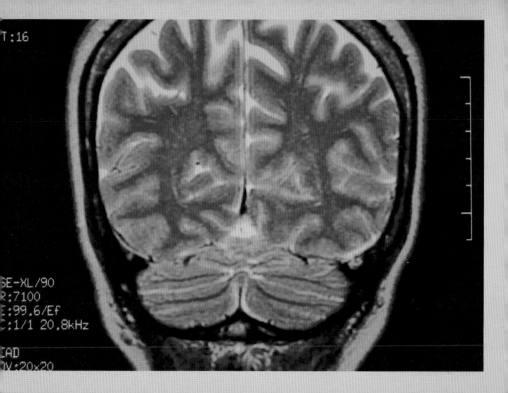

Programme 3 :
EXPLORING THE GOD QUESTION -
MIND AND CONSCIOUSNESS (PART 1)

WHAT IS AT STAKE IN THIS PROGRAMME...

... is whether the existence of human consciousness including spiritual and moral consciousness - points to a mind behind the universe.

INTRODUCING MIND AND CONSCIOUSNESS

(This introduction is reproduced in the Study Guide)

In the first programme, we probed some of the mysteries of our universe including the significance of finely balanced forces that permit life to exist. We debated whether such sophistication might be just 'luck' or, instead, points to an organising mind behind the universe.

In the second programme, we investigated the sheer wonder of life on earth and explored – and critiqued – the insights offered by Charles Darwin about the processes that have created life's glorious diversity. We learned how the science of genetics has revealed the astonishing and creative mechanisms that sustain and reproduce life forms and queried if blind chance or a creator's intention appears the more likely explanation.

In programme 3, we focus on the wonders of the human mind and brain. We ask if their awesome power to make us conscious, to allow us to think, to create and to reach out for ultimate explanations might be the product of natural processes alone; or, instead, provide the means through which we can discover, and relate to, the creator.

GENERAL AIMS

- To reflect on the mystery of human consciousness

- To consider if the existence of human consciousness might offer evidence for the existence of God

- To evaluate accounts of 'God consciousness'

AIMS FOR PART 1

- To encounter the wonders of the human brain and mind

- To recognise various levels of human consciousness including, in some cases, consciousness of God

- To consider if God consciousness – particularly as expressed in religions – can have a merely cultural explanation

- To reflect on whether our sense of morality derives from God or is a form of social pragmatism

56

SYNOPSIS – A LEADER'S GUIDE TO THE NARRATIVE

(There is a separate content guide in the Study Guide for the use of group members during viewing.)

- The human brain has been described as the most awesome phenomenon in the universe. It has the astonishing ability to work at both a conscious and a subconscious level.

- Human consciousness goes beyond our awareness of the physical world: there are higher levels of consciousness. These are central to all world religions.

- Often the arts, including music, can lead us to sense higher levels of consciousness.

- The origin and source of consciousness remains a deep mystery. A widely accepted view is that it must be produced from the brain which itself is a product of evolution. Others find it completely unconvincing that mind could emerge from a mindless process and argue that consciousness might have an origin and source beyond the human brain.

- Across the world, human beings express consciousness of a spiritual reality beyond themselves. These expressions are often found in religious worship and ritual.

- Atheists maintain such practices are little more than superstition and cultural conditioning. Yet, the systematic efforts of atheist states to eliminate religion have proved largely unsuccessful, pointing to the probability that the human sense of God cannot easily be quelled.

- Theists argue that, despite their differences, religions have more in common than divides them and that this is a highly significant factor in considering evidence for the existence of God.

- Although religions might seem to have common purposes, there remains the challenge of identifying truth among many diverse views.

- There is further evidence to be explored in the existence of the human sense of right and wrong. Atheists argue that, although by nature we are selfish, we are clever enough to have learned that our best interests are sometimes served by being co-operative; but theists counter that morality is direct evidence of human beings being created in the image of God.

Programme 3 :

EXPLORING THE GOD QUESTION — MIND AND CONSCIOUSNESS (PART 1)

PREPARING FOR VIEWING

God consciousness is a central idea in this programme. Before viewing, group members might share their views on the subject. What do they think is meant by 'God consciousness'? Does anyone have any experience of it? Is it a completely new idea? Does it seem absurd? What might count as evidence? By contrast, are there group members who believe that we can only rely on things that can be scientifically demonstrated to be true?

VIEWING THE PROGRAMME

Group members might wish to use the programme content guide in their booklet while viewing.

SEPARATING FACT FROM OPINION

While viewing the programmes and addressing the discussion questions it will be useful to distinguish between:

- statements of fact
- interpretation of facts
- opinion based more on intuition than evidence

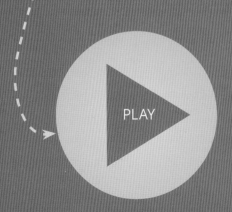

PLAY

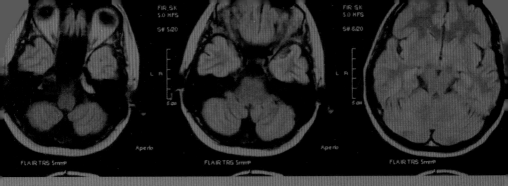

AFTER VIEWING THE PROGRAMME

As a reminder, Part 1 of the programme:

- Began by introducing the wonders of brain and mind and the amazing phenomenon of human consciousness. The origin of mind and consciousness is a deep mystery.

- Next, the documentary investigated ways in which human beings express or explore feelings of spirituality.

- Thereafter, the programme focused on religion and examined the possibility that it might originate from culture and superstition.

- However, others argue that it is highly significant that religion is so widespread across the world and that this indicates clearly that human beings tend to have a sense of a spiritual reality outside of themselves. Might we even be 'hard wired' to connect with this reality?

- If that reality is God, might that explain why human beings have a clear sense of right and wrong?

In this context, the characteristic debate between theists and atheists continues.

INITIAL REACTIONS

1 What is your overall initial reaction to the programme?

2 Did any aspect of the programme stand out for you – eg, was there some important new information? Or did something confirm or alter your view on the God question? Was there a statement that you found enlightening – or even infuriating?

3 Consider the view that you currently have about whether or not God exists. Did you find your view seriously challenged by contributors to the programme who have a different opinion?

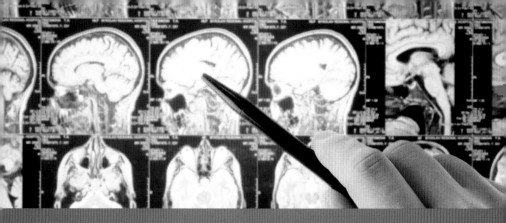

THE BIG ISSUES
(reproduced in Study Guide)

DOES THE **MYSTERY** AND THE **POWER** OF **HUMAN CONSCIOUSNESS** CONTRIBUTE MEANINGFULLY TO THE DEBATE ABOUT **GOD'S EXISTENCE?**

DOES THE WIDESPREAD POPULARITY OF **RELIGION** OFFER **EVIDENCE** THAT THERE IS A **SUPERNATURAL REALITY** OR IS THIS MORE A SIGN OF HUMAN **WISHFUL THINKING,** A **SUPERSTITIOUS PAST** AND EXPRESSIONS OF **VULNERABILITY?**

CAN HUMAN BEINGS BE **'GOOD' WITHOUT GOD?**

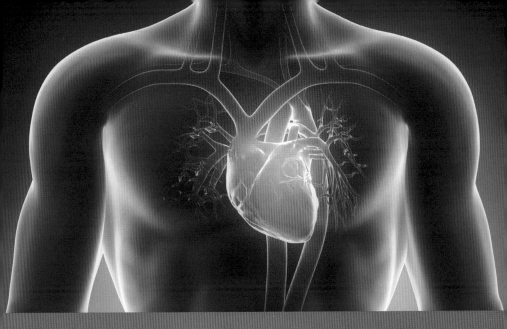

QUESTIONS FOR MORE IN-DEPTH DISCUSSION

Follow Questions 1–7 in the Study Guide

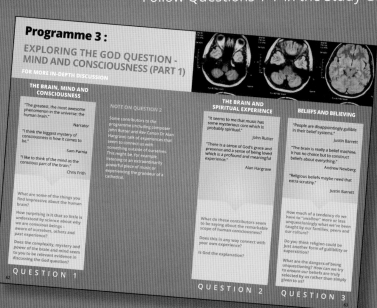

Programme 3 :

EXPLORING THE GOD QUESTION - MIND AND CONSCIOUSNESS (PART 1)

FOR MORE IN-DEPTH DISCUSSION

THE BRAIN, MIND AND CONSCIOUSNESS

"The greatest, the most awesome phenomenon in the universe: the human brain."

Narrator

"I think the biggest mystery of consciousness is how it comes to be."

Sam Parnia

"I like to think of the mind as the conscious part of the brain."

Chris Frith

What are some of the things you find impressive about the human brain?

How surprising is it that so little is understood by science about why we are conscious beings - aware of ourselves, others and past experience?

Does the complexity, mystery and power of the brain and mind seem to you to be relevant evidence in discussing the God question?

QUESTION 1

62

NOTE ON QUESTION 2

Some contributors to the programme (including composer John Rutter and Rev Canon Dr Alan Hargrave) talk of experiences that seem to connect us with something outside of ourselves. This might be, for example, listening to an extraordinarily powerful piece of music or experiencing the grandeur of a cathedral.

THE BRAIN AND SPIRITUAL EXPERIENCE

"It seems to me that music has some mysterious core which is probably spiritual."

John Rutter

"There is a sense of God's grace and presence and a sense of being loved which is a profound and meaningful experience."

Alan Hargrave

What do these contributors seem to be saying about the remarkable scope of human consciousness?

Does this in any way connect with your own experience?

Is God the explanation?

QUESTION 2

BELIEFS AND BELIEVING

"People are disappointingly gullible in their belief systems."

Justin Barrett

"The brain is really a belief machine. It has no choice but to construct beliefs about everything."

Andrew Newberg

"Religious beliefs maybe need that extra scrutiny."

Justin Barrett

How much of a tendency do we have to "swallow" more or less unquestioningly what we've been taught by our families, peers and our culture?

Do you think religion could be just another form of gullibility or superstition?

What are the dangers of being unquestioning? How can we try to ensure our beliefs are truly selected by us rather than simply given to us?

QUESTION 3

63

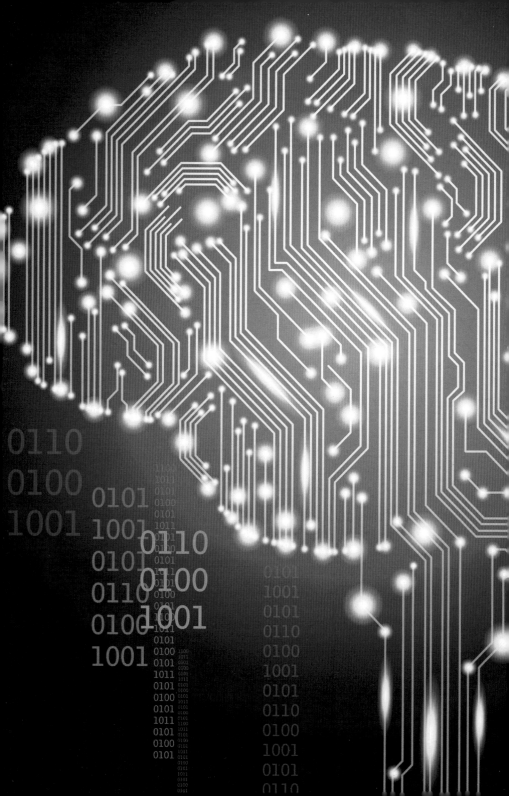

Programme 3:
EXPLORING THE GOD QUESTION - MIND AND CONSCIOUSNESS (PART 2)

WHAT IS AT STAKE IN THIS PROGRAMME...

...IS WHETHER THE EXISTENCE OF HUMAN CONSCIOUSNESS - INCLUDING SPIRITUAL AND MORAL CONSCIOUSNESS - POINTS TO A MIND BEHIND THE UNIVERSE.

SPECIFICALLY IN PART 2...

Is there reliable and valid evidence in human experience that points to spiritual reality and the existence of God?

63

AIMS FOR PART 2

- To examine various personal accounts of God consciousness

- To consider the validity of personal experiences as evidence for the existence of God

- To reflect on whether accounts of Near Death Experience (NDE) offer credible evidence of the immaterial mind and the material brain each having their own independent existence

- To encourage viewers to draw a conclusion about the extent to which consciousness, God consciousness and NDE can make a contribution to answering the God question

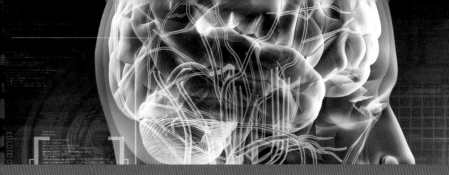

SYNOPSIS – A LEADER'S GUIDE TO THE NARRATIVE

(There is a separate content guide in the Study Guide for the use of group members during viewing.)

- Although much of the debate about the God question centres on science, there is also important evidence to be examined in personal experience.

- Father Matthew Green describes the nature of his God consciousness.

- Scientists have been testing the hypothesis that spirituality might depend to a large extent on the operation of a specific gene they have nicknamed the God gene. However other scientists are very sceptical of this explanation.

- Nevertheless, science continues to investigate the nature of spiritual experience and an important worldwide study is focusing on what can be learned from patients who have reported Near Death Experience (NDE) while clinically brain dead.

- NDE investigations are significant in attempting to identify if mind and consciousness continue after the point of clinical brain death. If tests are positive, then it is possible, or even likely, that consciousness does not originate in the brain but is a separate entity.

- Don Piper recounts his experience during a time when he was pronounced dead.

- The fascinating question is whether these experiences are 'real'. Atheists and theists provide their contrasting interpretations of the evidence.

- Silvia Glover of Brooklyn Tabernacle and some inmates of a Texas high security prison describe ways in which they believe God has changed their lives: impossible if he does not exist. Again, atheists and theists provide their contrasting views.

- In the end, a decision must be made about whether consciousness is evidence of God or exclusively a product of nature.*

---

* A summary of 'The Case for Theism' and 'The Case for Atheism' is provided as an Appendix within the Study Guide at the end of Part 2 Mind and Consciousness.

Programme 3 :

EXPLORING THE GOD QUESTION - MIND AND CONSCIOUSNESS (PART 2

PREPARING FOR VIEWING

Remind the group that Part 1 of the programme:

- ...began by introducing the wonders of the human brain and the amazing phenomenon of human consciousness.

- But for many, consciousness extends beyond day to day awareness of ourselves and other people to a different form of consciousness that many people across the world would describe as consciousness of God. The key issue is whether or not this consciousness is real evidence for God's existence or more a form of superstition and wishful thinking.

- Some argue that the human mind and brain are the products of blind evolutionary forces but others argue that the existence of the human sense of morality points in a different direction.

If time permits, re-cap on some of the key points, issues or controversies arising from the previous session.

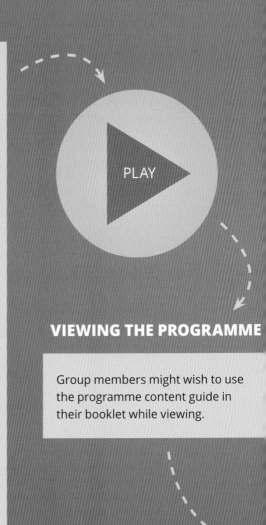

PLAY

VIEWING THE PROGRAMME

Group members might wish to use the programme content guide in their booklet while viewing.

As a reminder, Part 2 of the programme:

- ...examined a personal account of experiencing God spiritually within human consciousness. There have been attempts to explain this in biological terms with the identification of a so-called 'God gene' but the idea that spiritual consciousness can be attributed to a gene has been widely criticised.

- Science continues to investigate the source of human consciousness and a worldwide study is focusing on near death experience reported by a significant minority of people who have been assessed as clinically dead and thereafter successfully resuscitated. The key question is: have they experienced a reality beyond death or is hallucination a better explanation?

- Finally, there are personal testimonies of transformed lives.

Atheists argue that this is a form of self delusion but those involved express absolute conviction that, without the power of God, they would otherwise have been helpless to change.

INITIAL REACTIONS

1 What is your overall initial reaction to the programme?

2 What aspect of the programme stood out for you – for example, was there some important new information? Or did something confirm or alter your view on the God question? Was there a statement that you found enlightening – or even infuriating?

3 Consider the view that you currently have about whether or not God exists. Did you find your view seriously challenged by contributors to the programme who have a different opinion?

THE BIG ISSUES

(reproduced in Study Guide)

? WHAT **CREDIBILITY** CAN BE GIVEN TO ACCOUNTS ABOUT **PERSONAL EXPERIENCE OF GOD?** WHICH ASPECTS OF THE TESTIMONIES GIVEN IN THE PROGRAMME SEEM **BELIEVABLE/LESS BELIEVABLE?**

? HAVE **NEAR DEATH EXPERIENCES** ANY RELEVANCE TO THE GOD QUESTION?

? WHAT LIGHT CAN **SCIENCE** SHED ON CLAIMS OF **SPIRITUAL EXPERIENCE/SPIRITUAL REALITY?** WILL **SCIENCE** EVER BE ABLE TO **PROVIDE ALL THE ANSWERS?**

? SHOULD **GOD GET THE CREDIT** FOR THE **TRANFORMED LIVES** OF BELIEVERS?

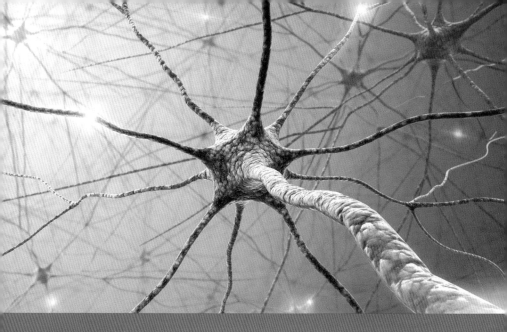

QUESTIONS FOR MORE
IN-DEPTH DISCUSSION

Follow Questions 1–6 in the Study Guide

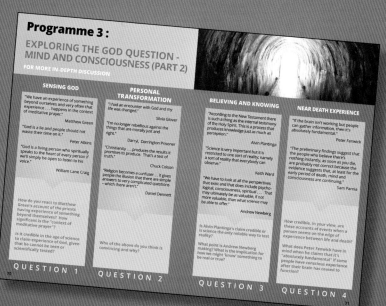

Programme 3 :

EXPLORING THE GOD QUESTION - MIND AND CONSCIOUSNESS (PART 2)
FOR MORE IN-DEPTH DISCUSSION

SENSING GOD

"We have an experience of something beyond ourselves and very often that experience . . . happens in the context of meditative prayer."

Matthew Green

"God is a lie and people should not waste their time on it."

Peter Atkins

"God is a living person who spiritually speaks to the heart of every person if we'll simply be open to listen to his voice."

William Lane Craig

How do you react to Matthew Green's account of the priests having experience of something beyond themselves? How significant is the "context of meditative prayer"?

Is it credible in the age of science to claim experience of God, given that he cannot be seen or scientifically tested?

QUESTION 1

PERSONAL TRANSFORMATION

"I had an encounter with God and my life was changed."

Silvia Glover

"I'm no longer rebellious against the things that are morally just and right."

Darryl, Darrington Prisoner

"Christianity . . . produces the results it promises to produce. That's a test of truth."

Chuck Colson

"Religion becomes a confuser . . . it gives people the illusion that there are simple answers to very complicated questions – which there aren't."

Daniel Dennett

Who of the above do you think is convincing and why?

QUESTION 2

BELIEVING AND KNOWING

"According to the New Testament there is such a thing as the internal testimony of the Holy Spirit. This is a process that produces knowledge just as much as perception."

Alvin Plantinga

"Science is very important but it is restricted to one sort of reality: namely a sort of reality that everybody can observe."

Keith Ward

"We have to look at all the perspectives that exist and that does include psychological, consciousness, spiritual . . . That may ultimately be as valuable, if not more valuable, than what science may be able to offer."

Andrew Newberg

Is Alvin Plantinga's claim credible or is science the only reliable way to test reality?

What point is Andrew Newberg making? What is the implication for how we might 'know' something to be real or true?

QUESTION 3

NEAR DEATH EXPERIENCE

"If the brain isn't working but people can gather information, then it's absolutely fundamental."

Peter Fenwick

"The preliminary findings suggest that the people who believe there's nothing instantly, as soon as you die, are probably not correct because the evidence suggests that, at least for the early period of death, mind and consciousness are continuing."

Sam Parnia

How credible, in your view, are these accounts of events when a person seems on the edge of experience between life and death?

What does Peter Fenwick have in mind when he claims that it's "absolutely fundamental" if some people have conscious experience after their brain has ceased to function?

QUESTION 4

AT THE END OF THE STUDY

Leaders, in drawing the study to a close, might invite group members to say if their initial views have been modified, weakened or strengthened by their experience during the study. How vigorously would they defend their view? Does doubt play a part? If God exists, what are the implications for our lives?

FEEDBACK

The producers always welcome feedback. Please express comments via the website, below.

USEFUL RESOURCES AND LINKS

Please refer to the Study Guide for Reading Lists and related weblinks.

UPDATES

Keep checking the website for the latest updates and fresh resource material:

www.thegodquestion.tv/explore